Cornerstones of Freedom

The Story of
THE POWERS OF THE PRESIDENT

By R. Conrad Stein

Illustrated by Keith Neely

CHILDRENS PRESS ™

CHICAGO

Library of Congress Cataloging in Publication Data

Stein, R. Conrad.
   The story of the powers of the president.

   (Cornerstones of freedom)
   Includes index.
   Summary: Describes the special powers invested in the
presidential office and discusses the use of these powers
by individual presidents throughout United States' history.
   1.   Executive power—United States—Juvenile literature.
2.   Presidents—United States—Juvenile literature.
[1.   Executive power.   2.   Presidents]   I.   Neely, Keith,
1943-   ill.   II.   Title.   III.   Series.
JK517.S73   1985   353.03'22   84-29257
ISBN 0-516-04684-5   AACR2

On the clear, crisp morning of October 14, 1962, a peculiar-looking aircraft with an unusually long wingspan crossed the skies high above Cuba. It was an American U-2 spy plane designed to make high-altitude photoreconnaissance flights. As the plane soared silently over the western shores of the island, the pilot switched on the complex photography equipment. Cameras carried by the U-2 were so sensitive that even from ten miles above they could spot a golf ball resting on an open green.

After the U-2 landed, pictures taken during this routine spy flight revealed a shocking construction project underway in the Cuban forests. Workers there were building special launching pads that could be used only for the firing of ballistic missiles capable of carrying nuclear warheads. The photos also showed neat rows of tents that housed the construction crew. Near the tents was a newly created soccer field. The field was significant because though Cubans loved baseball, they rarely played soccer. Their Russian allies, however, were avid soccer players.

The photos were rushed to American President John F. Kennedy. The world plunged into a frightening episode—the Cuban Missile Crisis.

On October 22, 1962, President Kennedy delivered a televised speech to the nation. First he announced that the Russians were placing missiles dangerously close to United States shores. He went on to say: "This urgent transformation of Cuba into an important strategic base. . .constitutes an explicit threat to the peace and security of all the Americas." He told the stunned viewers that he had ordered American warships to stop and search all vessels approaching Cuba. He called for the "prompt

dismantling and withdrawal of all offensive weapons in Cuba. . . ." The president hinted that he would take more-drastic military action if the missiles remained.

In the days following Kennedy's speech, American military forces hummed with activity. Secretly the president ordered the marines to prepare to land on Cuban beaches. He gave the air force a list of bombing targets on the island. A directive issued by the president put airfields, ships, and missile bases around the world on alert. The Russians took similar steps. The two superpowers stood poised like boxers in a ring. One of Kennedy's advisers described the confrontation with the words "We are eyeball to eyeball."

Finally, Nikita Khrushchev, premier of Soviet Russia, backed down. He agreed to remove the missiles in exchange for an American pledge not to invade Cuba. The Cuban Missile Crisis, which could have exploded into a nuclear holocaust, was over.

Kennedy's actions during the crisis serve as a dramatic example of the powers of the president. The American leader brought his country to the brink of what would certainly be the most destructive war in all human history. Yet the United States Constitution clearly gives Congress the sole power to declare war. A war-making ability is just one of the many powers the president has acquired since the office was first established.

In its infancy, the United States had no office of the presidency. After the country won its independence from Great Britain, the various states were guided by a code of laws called the Articles of Confederation. Under those laws, presidential functions were carried out by committees appointed by Congress.

The Articles of Confederation had many faults. Hoping to revise them, delegates from the various states met at Independence Hall in Philadelphia in 1787. There they decided to set aside the old Articles of Confederation and establish a new plan of government. The meeting became known as the Constitutional Convention, and the delegates proceeded to write the most important document in American history — the Constitution of the United States.

When creating the new office of the presidency, the delegates argued for days and nights. Most of them wanted a strong national leader because they believed that the failure to provide such a post was a major weakness of the Articles of Confederation.

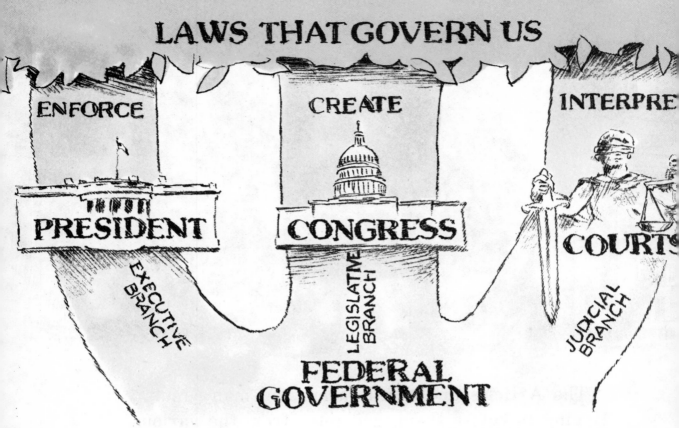

LAWS THAT GOVERN US

ENFORCE   **CREATE**   **INTERPRET**

PRESIDENT   **CONGRESS**   **COURTS**

EXECUTIVE BRANCH   LEGISLATIVE BRANCH   JUDICIAL BRANCH

FEDERAL GOVERNMENT

Only ten years earlier, however, those same delegates had fought a war against the powerful, one-man rule of the king of England. So they faced a perplexing question. How could they create a sufficiently strong office of the presidency, yet somehow keep that power in check?

After much debate, the delegates established a presidential office, but limited its authority by granting off-setting powers to other branches of the government. The Constitutional Convention divided the federal government into three distinct branches —the executive, the legislative, and the judicial.

The executive branch was represented by the president. Its job was to enforce, or execute, the laws. The president is often called the chief executive.

The legislative branch was represented by the two houses of Congress—the Senate and the House of Representatives. Its job was to create laws.

The judicial branch was represented by the court system headed by the Supreme Court. Its job was to interpret laws.

The arrangement was known as the separation of powers. The delegates believed that by dividing the authority, no one branch could become too powerful. Also, the delegates hoped, each branch would serve as a watchdog over the others. This built-in safeguard was called the system of checks and balances.

The most important powers the Constitution gave to the chief executive are the following: He is the commander-in-chief of the armed forces. He may grant pardons to people who commit crimes against the United States, except in the case of impeachment. He may, "with the advice and consent of the Senate," make treaties with foreign powers. He may appoint ambassadors to foreign countries, appoint justices to the Supreme Court, and appoint other high-ranking officers; however all these appointment privileges are subject to Senate approval. He may, "on extraordinary occasions," convene or adjourn Congress. Finally, he has the right to veto laws passed by Congress, though Congress may override his veto with a two-thirds vote.

The Constitution granted Congress much broader powers than it allowed the president. Most historians agree that the delegates intended to make Congress the most important branch of the government. The convention members, however, wrote the Constitution in general terms to give it flexibility. As James Madison, a delegate and future president, said: "In framing a system which we wish to last for ages, we should not lose sight of the changes which ages will produce."

A brief history of the presidency shows that the men who held that office have taken great liberties with the general terms of the Constitution.

Of the three branches of government, none has a greater ability to make a quick decision than the executive. This became clear as early as the Washington administration. George Washington took a proposed treaty with Great Britain to the

Senate seeking its "advice and consent." The Senate hemmed and hawed and argued endlessly. Meanwhile, Washington, who was known to have a temper, grew furious. Finally, he ordered his ministers to make the treaty with Great Britain. He then presented the finished package to the Senate as if to say: "Here it is; take it or leave it!" The embarrassed senators eventually approved the treaty.

Washington's actions demonstrated the efficiency of the office of the presidency. The president was able to act while Congress was lost in debate. The authors of the Constitution intended treaty-making to be a function shared by the president and the Senate, but every president since George Washington has dominated the process.

Chief executives following Washington continued to enhance the power of their office at the expense of the legislative branch. Many Congressmen claimed that Thomas Jefferson, the third president, acted

beyond his constitutional powers when he approved
a treaty to buy the Louisiana Territory from France
in 1803. Nothing in the Constitution permits the
president to buy land. Still, Jefferson claimed that
the Louisiana Purchase was merely a logical exten-
sion of his treaty-making powers. Andrew Jackson,
the seventh president, sent troops and warships to
Charleston, North Carolina, to enforce federal tariff
laws. He, too, was called a dictator by congressional
enemies; but Jackson maintained that he had acted
within the framework of the Constitution.

15

Strong presidents such as Jackson and Jefferson relied heavily on what are called the implied powers of the Constitution. These are powers that the Constitution suggests, rather than spells out. For example, the president must enforce laws. Sometimes law enforcement requires the use of troops. Therefore, the chief executive has the implied power to send soldiers wherever he deems it necessary to uphold the law.

The president's right to act as commander-in-chief of the army and navy carries with it a flood of implied powers. The revered President Abraham Lincoln employed his commander-in-chief authority to make his office so mighty that it would have shocked the original authors of the Constitution.

No president entered office under more perilous circumstances than did Abraham Lincoln. On the day he began his first term, seven Southern states had already seceded from the Union. A month later, Fort Sumter was fired upon, and the United States exploded into a bloody civil war.

Acting as commander-in-chief, Lincoln ordered the navy to blockade Southern ports. He expanded the army beyond the limits set by Congress. He allowed military police to arrest Southern sympathizers and hold them in jail without trial. Lincoln took these steps without waiting for the approval of the legislative or the judicial branches of government. During the long and turbulent Civil War years, he ruled like a dictator. Yet Lincoln had great respect for the Constitution. He believed that his drastic measures were necessary to preserve the country. "Was it possible to lose the nation and yet preserve the Constitution?" Lincoln asked. "By general law, life and limb must be protected, yet often a limb must be amputated to save a life; but a life is never wisely given to save a limb."

After Lincoln's death, the power of the president entered a period of decline. Historians often point out that drastic circumstances enhance presidential power. No significant crises rocked the land in the years immediately following the Civil War, and a series of comparatively weak presidents occupied the White House. But by the turn of the century, for the first time in its history the United States had become a world power. Then the authority of the chief executive soared once more.

Theodore Roosevelt became president in 1901, and served until 1909. He warned European nations not to interfere in the affairs of Latin America. He also

led a fight to limit the huge American corporations. These were unusual extensions of presidential authority during peacetime. Woodrow Wilson was president during World War I. After the war ended, he made the presidency an international office by helping to form the League of Nations.

Franklin Delano Roosevelt was elected in 1932 in the midst of a great economic depression. Thousands of unemployed workers stood for hours in lines hoping to bring home something to feed their families. Businessmen boarded up their plants for lack of work. City dwellers lost their homes and farmers lost their land because they could not make mortgage payments. Yet, during his first inaugural address, Franklin Roosevelt told the nation, "...first of all, let me assert my firm belief that the only thing we have to fear is fear itself. ..." He then launched a bold program called the New Deal. It started massive government projects designed to create jobs and stimulate the economy.

The New Deal soon developed enemies in the judicial branch. A conservative Supreme Court declared many New Deal acts to be unconstitutional. Roosevelt struck back by sponsoring a bill that would allow him to appoint additional justices to the Supreme Court. Although the bill never passed Congress, the mere threat of presidential domination caused many of the justices to become suddenly sympathetic to New Deal measures.

Roosevelt was president during the darkest hours of World War II. Like Lincoln, he assumed great wartime powers. Under his secret orders, a multi-million-dollar program aimed at exploding the world's first atomic bomb was launched. Only a few members of Congress knew about the massive project.

Roosevelt did not always use his wartime powers wisely. Early during the conflict, hysterical Californians demanded that all persons of Japanese ancestry be removed from the West Coast because they were suspected of spying. Even though there was not a shred of evidence that Japanese-Americans were spies, Roosevelt issued an executive order that placed all West Coast Japanese in dismal detention camps for the duration of the war.

After World War II, the fear of Communist expansion gripped the country. This tension led to two devastating wars. In 1950, President Truman sent American troops to South Korea to counter a North Korean invasion. A long and costly war

followed. Four presidents—Dwight Eisenhower, John Kennedy, Lyndon Johnson, and Richard Nixon—contributed to promoting the Vietnam War. Under Lyndon Johnson, that war reached its peak with the involvement of more than half a million American fighting men. Never once did a president ask Congress to declare war on North Korea or the enemy forces in Vietnam. They were both presidential wars fought on the authority of the chief executive's rights as commander-in-chief.

In addition to his broad powers as commander-in-chief, the modern president is strengthened by his role as party leader, his ability to command the public's attention, and the ever-growing use of what are called executive agreements.

Today the president is head of his political party. This position adds to the power of his office. House members and Senators often vote along party lines. Consequently, the president, as a party leader, can influence votes in the legislative branch. In addition, he can introduce bills through party channels. Party leadership also strengthens his veto power. Overriding a presidential veto requires a two-thirds vote of both the Senate and the House. This is nearly impossible to attain when the president's party votes along the lines he suggests. Often the mere threat of a veto is enough to force legislators to reconsider a bill.

The president is also a public figure who commands the attention of the news media. During the Great Depression, Franklin Delano Roosevelt hosted regular radio shows called "fireside chats" that told the people what his administration was doing to eliminate the ravages of poverty. John Kennedy displayed his razor-sharp grasp of the issues by holding presidential news conferences on live television. Ronald Reagan, a former Hollywood actor, is a master performer in front of television cameras.

Many Americans wish to idolize their president, much as people of earlier times wanted to revere their kings and queens. The mere glamor of the office adds to its prestige. The president may, on occasion, go over the heads of Congress and appeal directly to the people about an issue.

In foreign policy matters, the president's authority has been enhanced by the frequent use of executive agreements between nations. As the name implies, these are agreements between executive branches. For example, the American president could make an agreement with the president of Mexico calling for diligent border patrols to catch drug smugglers. Executive agreements are similar to treaties, but they do not require the approval of a two-thirds vote in the Senate. Consequently, they can be concluded with a handshake. Executive agreements can also be made in secret if the circumstances require.

Given the vast powers of the president, it is fair to ask whether the system of checks and balances is still working. Are the legislative and judicial branches meaningless in comparison to the awesome powers of the executive? Are we are now governed by the president alone?

Presidential rule remains an overwhelming force, but recently the other branches have moved to curb executive authority.

The conflict in Vietnam was the most unpopular war America has fought during this century. It was almost entirely a presidential war, fought under the commander-in-chief clause in the Constitution. However, the Constitution gives the legislative branch the authority to finance all government projects, including wars. By simply refusing to vote funds to sustain the war, Congress could have ended the conflict. But while the Vietnam War raged, Congress made no such effort.

In 1973, Congress passed the War Powers Act which, in theory, cuts off funding for future presidential wars. President Nixon vetoed the War Powers Act, but Congress overrode his veto. So far, three presidents have bent the rules of the act. President Ford ordered troops to capture the *Mayaguez,* an American freighter seized by the Cambodians. President Carter, in 1980, sent special forces to Iran in a vain attempt to rescue hostages held by that country. In 1983, President Reagan ordered a full-scale invasion of the Caribbean island of Grenada. Each of these actions was a quick strike, and the presidents involved claimed that they had not violated the spirit of the War Powers Act.

It is still not clear whether the War Powers Act could prevent a prolonged presidential war such as the one in Vietnam. Many experts believe that the president's war-making ability is too strong for Congress to keep in check. Political scientist James MacGregor Burns wonders: "Will [Congress] have the courage to resist being stampeded into granting power whenever a president waves the flag and says there is an urgent crisis? The history of presidential actions in wartime suggests that presidents in the future will not have much difficulty in doing pretty much what they please. The Constitution, as Chief Justice Hughes once said, is a 'fighting Constitution.' "

Historically, the judicial branch is the weakest of the three departments of the federal government. But in 1974, the Supreme Court asserted its authority over the chief executive when it ordered President Nixon to surrender tape recordings related to the break-in at the Watergate Hotel in Washington. That burglary triggered the biggest political scandal in American history. At first, Nixon refused to give up the tapes. He claimed that as chief executive it was his privilege to keep certain documents a secret. The court held that not even the president is above the law and forced Nixon to surrender the tapes.

The ultimate power the other branches have over the executive branch is the ability to remove the president from office by the impeachment process. The Constitution gives the Congress the right to impeach the president for "treason, bribery, or other high crimes and misdemeanors." So far in United States history no president has been convicted of an impeachable offense. In 1868, the Senate fell one vote shy of convicting President Andrew Johnson. In 1974, President Nixon, stung by the Watergate scandal, resigned before impeachment proceedings against him could begin. To date, he is the only chief executive ever to resign his office.

The bitter war in Vietnam and the Watergate scandal have led many Americans to believe that too much power has poisoned the office of the presidency. Presidential government, which was popular in the 1960s during the Cuban Missile Crisis, fell out of favor in the late 1970s. But the authority and prestige of the presidency have gone through periods of ups and downs before. Still, the office will

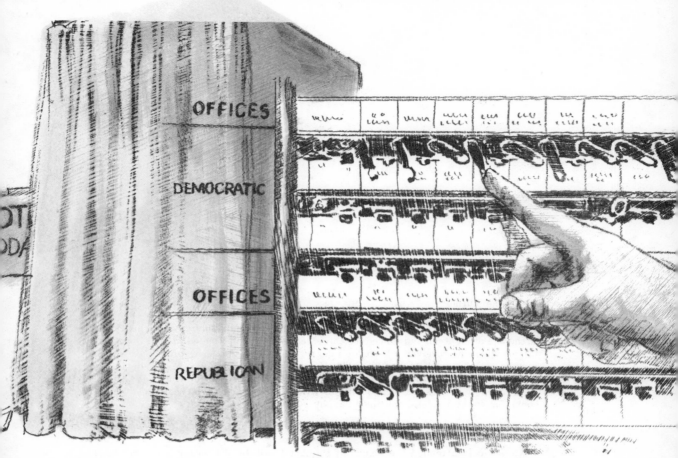

probably remain, as John Kennedy once said, "the vital center of action in our whole scheme of government."

Finally, the greatest curb on presidential power lies with the voters. Every four years, a new man or woman seeks the office, and often an incumbent president asks for another four-year term. Franklin Delano Roosevelt once gave this wise reminder to all presidents who came after him: "The president is commander-in-chief, [but] he, too, has his superior officer—the people of the United States."

About the Author

R. Conrad Stein was born and grew up in Chicago. He enlisted in the Marine Corps at the age of eighteen and served for three years. He then attended the University of Illinois where he received a bachelor's degree in history. He later studied in Mexico, earning an advanced degree from the University of Guanajuato. Mr. Stein is the author of many other books, articles, and short stories written for young people.

Mr. Stein now lives in Chicago with his wife, Deborah Kent, who is also a writer of books for young readers, and their daughter Janna.

About the Artist

Keith Neely attended the School of the Art Institute of Chicago and received a Bachelor of Fine Arts degree with honors from the Art Center College of Design where he majored in illustration. He has worked as an art director, designer, and illustrator and has taught advertising illustration and advertising design at Biola College in La Mirada, California. Mr. Neely is currently a freelance illustrator whose work has appeared in numerous magazines, books, and advertisements. He lives with his wife and five children in Florida.